Franklin's
Picture Dictionary

Kids Can Press

Based on the Franklin books by Paulette Bourgeois and Brenda Clark.
Written by Rosemarie Shannon, M. Ed.
Some interior illustrations prepared with the assistance of Shelley Southern,
based on original drawings by Brenda Clark.

Franklin

Franklin is a trademark of Kids Can Press Ltd.
The character Franklin was created by Paulette Bourgeois and Brenda Clark.
Text © 2004 Contextx Inc.
Illustrations © 2004 Brenda Clark Illustrator Inc.

Kids Can Press acknowledges the financial support of the Government of Ontario, through
the Ontario Media Development Corporation's Ontario Book Initiative; the Ontario Arts
Council; the Canada Council for the Arts; and the Government of Canada, through the
BPIDP, for our publishing activity.

Kids Can Press Ltd.
2250 Military Road
Tonawanda, NY 14150

www.kidscanpress.com

Edited by Jennifer Stokes
Designed by Sherill Chapman
Educational consultant: Maureen Skinner Weiner,
    United Synagogue Day School, Willowdale, Ontario

Printed and bound in Hong Kong, China, by Book Art Inc., Toronto
This book is smyth sewn casebound.

US 04 0 9 8 7 6 5 4 3 2 1

National Library of Canada Cataloguing in Publication Data

Shannon, Rosemarie
    Franklin's picture dictionary / Rosemarie Shannon ; illustrated by Shelley Southern.

American ed.
The character Franklin was created by Paulette bourgeois and Brenda Clark.
For children aged 5-8.

ISBN 1-55337-711-7

1. Picture dictionaries, English — Juvenile literature. I. Southern, Shelley II. Bourgeois,
Paulette III. Clark, Brenda IV. Title.

PE1629.S48 2004a   j423'.1   C2004-900014-4

Kids Can Press is a *lorus*™ Entertainment company

Contents

Resources for parents and teachers

Welcome to
Franklin's Picture Dictionary!

Meet Franklin and his friends.

Visit fun places in Woodland.

And learn about some of the things in Franklin's world.

Along the way, discover words that are new to you and find words that you already know.

Franklin and his friends look forward to seeing you often as you come back to this book again and again!

Note to adults:

For lots of language-learning ideas and suggestions for using this book with children, turn to page 102.

Aa

Franklin's adoring aunt arrived for an afternoon visit.

above

Hawk is flying high **above** Woodland.

add   *adds, added, adding*

Franklin is learning to **add** numbers.

afraid

Franklin is **afraid** of the strange noises he hears in the dark woods.

afternoon

What a perfect **afternoon** for fishing and bike riding!

again

Bear's tummy is always rumbling. Look, he's having a snack **again**!

airplane

This is Franklin's toy **airplane**.

alike

Goose and her mother look a lot **alike**.

all

Franklin is putting away **all** of his toys.

alone

When Moose was new at school, he stood **alone** during recess.

along

Chipmunk and Mouse are walking **along** the path.

always

Bear **always** hides in the berry patch when he plays hide-and-seek!

angry

Why is Franklin **angry**?

annoyed

Franklin is **annoyed**. He doesn't want to go outside!

another

Franklin would like **another** cookie.

apple *apples*

Franklin and Bear are eating **apples**.

art

Franklin's class is working on an **art** project.

ask *asks, asked, asking*

Franklin is **asking** his mother if Bear can sleep over.

asleep

Now that Bear is sound **asleep**, the tooth fairy can visit.

aunt

Franklin loves the gift he received from Great-**Aunt** Harriet.

awake

Bear can't sleep. He's still wide **awake**!

away

Franklin is putting **away** his blanket.

Bb

Bear brought his mother
a birthday breakfast in bed.

back

Franklin and Bear like to ride at the **back**
of the bus.

bad

Hmmph! Today is a **bad** day. There
isn't enough snow to go sledding.

badger

Badger uses crutches to help her walk.

bag

Franklin carries his school supplies in his **bag**.

bake *bakes, baked, baking*

Franklin's mother is **baking** a batch of cookies.

ball

This is Franklin's soccer **ball**.

bandage

Franklin needs to wear a **bandage** until the crack in his shell heals.

baseball

Franklin and his friends are playing **baseball**.

basket

Bear collects berries in his **basket**.

bath

Harriet is very dirty. She needs a **bath** with lots of soapy bubbles!

bear

Bear likes to play marbles.

beaver

Beaver is giving her mother a picture.

beside

Sometimes Franklin sits **beside** Beaver on the bus.

best

Franklin and Bear are **best** friends.

between

Franklin sits **between** his parents at the dinner table.

bicycle

Franklin is riding his new **bicycle**.

big

At first, Franklin was afraid of Moose because he is so **big**.

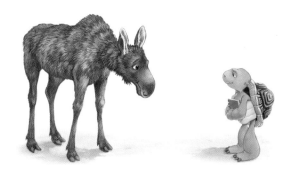

birthday

For his **birthday**, Franklin likes chocolate cake with ladybugs.

blanket

Franklin loves his old blue **blanket**.

blow *blows, blew, blowing*

Coach Porcupine **blows** her whistle to get the team's attention.

blueberry *blueberries*

Blueberries are Bear's favorite snack.

bone *bones*

Whose **bones** do these X rays show?

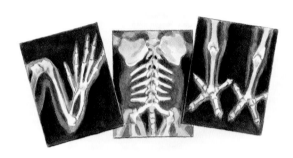

book *books*

Franklin loves to read his Dynaroo **books**.

bouquet

Great-Aunt Harriet sent a **bouquet** of flowers to Franklin's mother.

box

A **box** can make a great spaceship!

brave

Franklin tried to be **brave** even though he was afraid to get an X ray.

break *breaks, broke, breaking*

Uh-oh. Who **broke** Franklin's cup?

breakfast

Franklin eats Fly Krispy cereal for **breakfast**.

bridge

You have to cross the **bridge** to get to Bear's house.

brother

Harriet loves her big **brother**, Franklin.

bubble

Franklin is blowing a big **bubble**.

build *builds, built, building*

When it snows, Franklin **builds** snow turtles in his yard.

bus

Franklin and his friends ride the **bus** to school.

Cc

**Clothes, costumes and clutter —
time to clean the closet!**

cake

Granny is making a birthday **cake** for Franklin's mother.

call *calls, called, calling*

Franklin is **calling** Bear on the telephone.

camera

Franklin found a **camera**. Hmmm. Who does it belong to?

camp *camps, camped, camping*

Franklin and Bear are **camping** out in the living room.

can *cans*

Tin **cans** make great play telephones!

candle *candles*

When the lights go out during a storm, Franklin's mother lights **candles**.

candy

Franklin's father is enjoying his valentine **candy**.

cap

Franklin often wears his red baseball **cap**.

card

Who is this valentine **card** for?

carry
carries, carried, carrying

Franklin is sleepy. His father is **carrying** him home.

catch
catches, caught, catching

Franklin is about to **catch** the ball. He's also **catching** lots of flies!

castle

Sir Franklin built a **castle** out of blocks.

chair

Mr. Owl is sitting in his rocking **chair**.

cat

Beaver says that if she had a pet, it would be a **cat**.

cheese

Franklin is eating **cheese** while Raccoon takes his picture. "**Cheese**!"

chess

Mr. Heron is teaching Franklin and Badger to play the game of **chess**.

choose
chooses, chose, choosing

Franklin is **choosing** a costume for Halloween.

classroom

There are lots of fun things to do in the **classroom**!

clean
cleans, cleaned, cleaning

The orderly is **cleaning** the hospital floor.

clock

This **clock** hangs beside the fireplace in Franklin's kitchen.

cloud

Franklin knows that a dark **cloud** means rain!

clubhouse

Franklin and his friends have a **clubhouse** in a hollowed-out tree.

coach *coaches, coached, coaching*

Ms. Porcupine **coaches** Franklin's soccer team.

cold

Franklin wears his hat, scarf and mittens when it is **cold** outside.

cook *cooks, cooked, cooking*

Franklin is helping his father **cook** dinner.

cookie *cookies*

These bug-leaf **cookies** are freshly baked.

cool

The **cool** water feels great on a hot day.

corn

Franklin is shucking **corn** for the big Thanksgiving dinner.

crayon *crayons*

Franklin draws colorful pictures with his **crayons**.

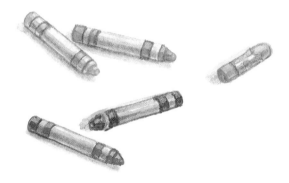

crown

Franklin wears this **crown** to play dress-up.

cry *cries, cried, crying*

Why is Franklin **crying**?

cup

Franklin's favorite **cup** has a picture of a train on it.

cut *cuts, cut, cutting*

Beaver **cut** out a string of paper ghosts.

Dd

Sir Franklin is dressed to defend Sir Lady Beaver from dangerous dragons.

dad

Franklin has lots of fun with his **dad**.

dance *dances, danced, dancing*

When he hears music, Franklin likes to **dance**.

dark

Franklin has a night-light so he won't be afraid of the **dark**.

day

Franklin can see that it's a bright, sunny **day**.

desk

Mr. Owl has a telephone on his **desk**.

deep

Franklin can swim **deep** underwater in the pond.

dig *digs, dug, digging*

Franklin's father is **digging** in the garden.

dentist

The **dentist** is checking Beaver's teeth.

dinner

Franklin's favorite **dinner** is fly pie and broccoli soup.

dinosaur

Franklin and his friends saw a **dinosaur** at the museum.

direction *directions*

This signpost points in all **directions**!

dirty

Uh-oh! Harriet is **dirty** — and so is Sam!

disappointed

Franklin is **disappointed** that he can't ride his bike without training wheels.

dive *dives, dived, diving*

Franklin is good at **diving** into the pond.

doctor

Bear's mother is a **doctor**. She takes care of everyone in Woodland.

dog

Franklin takes his toy **dog**, Sam, everywhere!

doll

Harriet left her favorite **doll** outside in the yard.

door

This is the **door** to Bear's house.

down

Franklin helps Harriet go **down** the slide.

draw *draws, drew, drawing*

Franklin **draws** wonderful pictures.

dream *dreams, dreamed, dreaming*

Franklin is **dreaming** about scoring the winning goal.

dress

Beaver wears a beautiful **dress** to play **dress**-up.

drum

Sometimes, Franklin plays the **drum** during music class.

drink

Franklin likes the special **drink** the nurse brought him at the hospital.

dry   *dries, dried, drying*

Franklin's mother helps him **dry** off after his bath.

drop   *drops, dropped, dropping*

Uh-oh! Franklin's valentines are **dropping** out of his bag.

duck   *ducks*

A family of **ducks** lives near the pond.

Ee

Franklin eagerly embraces
his elephant every evening.

eager

Franklin is **eager** to go on a class trip
to the museum.

early

Franklin wakes his parents **early** on
the first day of school.

easel

Franklin paints pictures on his **easel**.

easy

Beaver says it's **easy** to ride a bike without training wheels.

eat *eats, ate, eating*

Franklin and his friends are **eating** blueberry muffins. Yum!

edge

Duck is diving off the **edge** of the dock.

egg *eggs*

Franklin needs **eggs** to make fly pie.

empty

The box for the toy drive is **empty**. Soon, it will be filled with toys.

enjoy *enjoys, enjoyed, enjoying*

Beaver is **enjoying** her ice cream cone.

enough

Franklin has had **enough** to eat.
He finished the whole fly pie!

entrance

Franklin and his friends are waiting
at the museum **entrance**.

envelope

Franklin put his letter to the tooth fairy
in this **envelope**.

evening

The moon comes out in the **evening**.

everybody

Everybody ate Thanksgiving dinner
together under the big oak tree.

excited

Franklin was **excited** when Granny told
him he had a new baby sister.

Ff

It's Franklin's favorite food
— fresh fly pie!

fairy

The tooth **fairy** is leaving something for Fox.

family

Franklin's **family** has grown — now he has a little sister!

fast

Beaver is riding very **fast**.

father

Franklin's **father** is always there for him.

feather

Whose **feather** is this?

feed *feeds, fed, feeding*

Bear is helping Franklin **feed** Goldie.

fence

Fox, Beaver and Raccoon are hiding behind the **fence**.

fight

Raccoon and Skunk are having a friendly snowball **fight**!

find *finds, found, finding*

Franklin was surprised to **find** a camera in the bushes.

fire

Franklin's father built a **fire** for their camp-out.

firefighter

Franklin is pretending to be a **firefighter**.

fish

Goldie is Franklin's pet **fish**.

flashlight

Franklin is playing **flashlight** tag.

float *floats, floated, floating*

Rabbit and Goose are **floating** on the water.

floor

Franklin and Bear are camped out on the **floor**.

flower *flowers*

Oh, no! Harriet wants to eat the **flowers**!

fly *flies, flew, flying*

Hawk likes to **fly** loop-the-loops.

follow *follows, followed, following*

Beaver and Fox are **following** Franklin and Snail.

forest

Franklin and his class saw a rain **forest** on their trip to the museum.

fountain

This fish **fountain** is in Woodland's town square.

fox

Fox is one of Franklin's friends.

fresh

Franklin and Harriet are gathering **fresh** vegetables from the garden.

friend

Franklin made a new **friend** when Moose moved to Woodland.

frog *frogs*

Frogs live in the pond where Franklin swims.

full

The box for the toy drive is **full**.

fun

Pretending to be a pilot is **fun**!

funny

Franklin's **funny** faces make Harriet laugh.

Gg

Gosh!
Goose is a great goalie!

game

Franklin and Moose are playing a **game** of checkers.

garage

The fire truck is parked in its **garage**.

garbage

Uh-oh. Who left this **garbage** on the ground?

gate

Who left the **gate** open?

get   *gets, got, getting*

Franklin **got** lots of cards on Valentine's Day.

give   *gives, gave, giving*

Snail is **giving** his mother flowers for her birthday.

glasses

Franklin's father wears **glasses** to see better.

glove   *gloves*

When he works in the garden, Franklin's father wears **gloves**.

go   *goes, went, going*

Fox's mother told everyone to **go** indoors when it started to rain.

good

Yum! Those pies smell **good**!

good-bye

Franklin is waving **good-bye** to Moose.

grandparent *grandparents*

This is a picture of Franklin with his **grandparents**.

granny

Franklin likes to go for walks with his **granny**.

grouchy

Why is Franklin in a **grouchy** mood today?

grow *grows, grew, growing*

Franklin's father **grows** lots of different vegetables in his garden.

Hh

**Franklin is happy
to hold Harriet!**

Halloween

Every **Halloween**, Franklin's family puts a jack-o'-lantern on their front steps.

hammer

Mr. Mole is using his **hammer** to put up a sign.

hang *hangs, hung, hanging*

Bear can **hang** from the monkey bars, but Beaver is still learning.

happy

Franklin makes Harriet **happy**.

hard

At first, it was **hard** for Franklin to ride a bike without training wheels.

hat

Franklin is putting a **hat** on Badger's head.

heart *hearts*

On Valentine's Day, Mr. Owl decorated the classroom clock with **hearts**!

heavy

The sled is so **heavy** that everyone is helping to move it.

hello

Franklin and Bear are saying **hello**.

help
helps, helped, helping

Franklin is **helping** his father with the laundry.

here

Is Franklin's blanket in **here**?

hide
hides, hid, hiding

When Franklin is frightened, he **hides** in his shell.

high

Franklin loves to swing **high**.

hill

Franklin's school was built on top of a small **hill**.

hit
hits, hit, hitting

It took lots of practice for Fox to learn to **hit** a baseball.

hold *holds, held, holding*

Franklin feels safe when he **holds** his blanket.

hollow

Franklin is playing hide-and-seek. Is anyone hiding in this **hollow** log?

home

Beaver's **home** is in the pond. It's called a lodge.

honey

Bear loves **honey**.

hop *hops, hopped, hopping*

Rabbit can **hop** higher than anyone else.

horn

Franklin has a **horn** on his bicycle to warn others that he's coming.

hospital

This is the **hospital** in Woodland.

hot

Mmmm, steaming **hot** fly casserole!

house

Snail's **house** is very small.

hug *hugs, hugged, hugging*

Franklin feels better when his father **hugs** him.

hungry

Bear is always **hungry**!

hurry *hurries, hurried, hurrying*

Franklin is **hurrying** home to see his mother.

Ii

Stopping for ice cream is an incredibly irresistible idea!

ice

Hooray! The **ice** on the pond is thick enough for skating.

inside

Franklin sleeps **inside** his shell, where it is cozy and warm.

into

Franklin kicked the ball **into** the net!

J j

Franklin's mother makes
jars of jam and jelly every July.

jacket

Harriet needs help putting on her **jacket**.

jam

Franklin likes to put lots of fly-berry
jam on his toast.

jar

Beaver has a **jar** full of flies for Franklin.

jewelry

Franklin's mother has pretty **jewelry**.

jigsaw

Franklin is working on this **jigsaw** puzzle.

job

Franklin helps around the house. Today his **job** is to hang up the laundry.

joke

Fox is telling a **joke** that makes Franklin laugh.

juice

Franklin likes orange **juice** with his breakfast.

jump *jumps, jumped, jumping*

Franklin is **jumping** for joy.

K k

Keys and the kettle are kept in the kitchen.

kangaroo

Franklin's favorite hero is Dynaroo, a **kangaroo** who is super fast and strong.

keep *keeps, kept, keeping*

Franklin **keeps** special things in his scrapbook.

key *keys*

Aha! Franklin found his mother's missing **keys**!

kick *kicks, kicked, kicking*

Franklin likes to practice **kicking** the soccer ball.

kind

Franklin's **kind** friends are helping him up.

king

There is a portrait of a **king** at the museum.

kite

Franklin's **kite** is flying high.

knight

Sir Franklin is a loyal and brave **knight**.

know *knows, knew, knowing*

Beaver **knows** lots of things. What is she explaining to Franklin now?

Ll

Look at all the leaves on the lawn!

ladder

A **ladder** is useful for hanging curtains.

lamp

This **lamp** lights up Franklin's room.

large

Moose looks very **large** beside Franklin!

last

Franklin and Moose are the **last** ones to sit down for lunch.

learn *learns, learned, learning*

Franklin is **learning** to ride his bike without training wheels.

late

Franklin is in a hurry — he doesn't want to be **late** for Bear's party.

library

Everyone enjoys story time with Mrs. Goose at the **library**.

laugh *laughs, laughed, laughing*

Beaver is **laughing** because Franklin is slipping and sliding in the mud.

lick *licks, licked, licking*

Baking is fun — especially when Franklin gets to **lick** the icing off the spoon.

lie   *lies, lay, lying*

Mr. Mole is **lying** down because he doesn't feel well.

lift   *lifts, lifted, lifting*

The movers are **lifting** furniture off the truck.

lightning

Whenever you see **lightning**, you'll probably hear thunder, too!

line

Franklin and his friends are waiting in **line** for the school bus.

listen   *listens, listened, listening*

What was that? Franklin is **listening** carefully.

little

Snail is **little** compared to Franklin.

live
lives, lived, living

This is where Franklin **lives**.

long

Franklin's dress-up coat is very **long**.

look
looks, looked, looking

Franklin is **looking** at himself in the mirror.

loud

Harriet is so **loud** that Franklin's ears are hurting!

love
loves, loved, loving

Franklin **loves** his mother very much.

lunch

Franklin likes to have bug stew and salad for **lunch**.

Mmmm! Fresh muffins make a marvelous morning meal!

mad

Franklin is **mad**. Harriet has his toy dog, Sam!

mail

Franklin got a postcard in the **mail**. Who could it be from?

make *makes, made, making*

Franklin helped Harriet **make** her own doll.

many

Many friends joined Franklin's family for Thanksgiving dinner.

map

Mr. Owl is showing a **map** of Woodland to the class.

marble *marbles*

Franklin has some colorful **marbles** in his collection.

market

Franklin often visits the farmers' **market** on Saturday mornings.

mask *masks*

Doctors and nurses wear **masks** in the operating room.

mess

Franklin must tidy his room. It's a **mess**!

middle

Bear is walking between Rabbit and Franklin. He is in the **middle**.

money

Franklin keeps his **money** in a piggy bank.

mirror

Franklin is checking in the **mirror** to see how fearsome he looks.

monster

Look at Franklin's **monster** costume — he's Franklinstein!

mom

Franklin picked some flowers for his **mom**.

moon

Tonight, there's a crescent **moon** in the sky.

moose

Moose is Franklin's largest friend.

mother

Franklin is giving his **mother** a birthday hug.

mouse   *mice*

These **mice** live in a tiny **mouse** house.

mud

Oh, no. Harriet landed in a puddle of **mud** at the bottom of the slide!

museum

Franklin's class is on a trip to the **museum**.

music

Franklin and his friends are playing **music** at the school concert.

Nn

Rabbit's new notebook is filled with numerous numbers!

name

Beaver's **name** is on her plant project.

nap

Franklin is taking a **nap** inside his shell.

neat

Franklin put his things away in boxes. Now his room is **neat**.

necklace

Franklin made this macaroni **necklace** for his mother.

nest

Soon, this **nest** will be filled with baby birds.

neighbor *neighbors*

Franklin and his **neighbors** are going to have Thanksgiving dinner outdoors.

new

Franklin got a **new** book from the tooth fairy.

nervous

Franklin is **nervous** about acting in the school play.

newspaper

Franklin's father is reading the **newspaper**.

night

The tooth fairy comes to visit at **night**.

not

Franklin is lost. He should **not** be in the woods alone.

nobody

On his first day of school, Moose was worried that **nobody** would like him.

nothing

There's **nothing** left in the bowl! Who ate all the popcorn?

noise

Franklin is making so much **noise** that the mice cover their ears!

nurse

Nurse Cougar is taking care of Franklin at the hospital.

Oops! Franklin fell off
of his bike. Ouch!

o'clock

It's three **o'clock** on the frog clock.
Snack time!

office

Franklin is at the doctor's **office** for
a checkup.

often

Franklin's mother **often** bakes fly pie
for Franklin.

59

old

Franklin found an **old** truck in his toy box.

on

Snail rides **on** Franklin's shell when they have a long way to walk.

once

Franklin loves Halloween. Too bad it comes only **once** a year!

open

Uh-oh. Someone left the door **open**.

operation

Franklin needs an **operation** to fix his cracked shell.

orange *oranges*

Mmmm, fresh and juicy **oranges**!

other

Harriet is wearing only one boot. Where is the **other** one?

otter

Otter is Franklin's friend. She moved away, and now they're pen pals.

out

Franklin is emptying **out** his book bag. Where could his missing valentines be?

outside

Franklin is wondering what the weather is like **outside**.

over

Is that a real ghost flying **over** everyone's head?

owl

Mr. **Owl** is very wise. He teaches Franklin all kinds of things.

P p

Franklin is particularly proud
of the pictures he painted.

pack *packs, packed, packing*
Bear is **packing** his bag for
a sleepover at Franklin's house.

package *packages*
Postman Badger is delivering **packages**
from Great-Aunt Harriet.

page
Franklin likes to look at every **page**
in his scrapbook.

paint *paints, painted, painting*
Goose is **painting** a picture for her mother.

pair
Franklin has a new **pair** of boots.

paper
Franklin cut some flowers out of **paper**.

parent *parents*
Sometimes, both of Franklin's **parents** meet him at the bus stop.

park
Porcupine likes to go in-line skating at the **park**.

party
Everyone is having lots of fun at the Halloween **party**!

peekaboo

Harriet loves to play **peekaboo** with Franklin.

pencil *pencils*

Franklin has lots of coloring **pencils**.

pet

Goose says that if she had a **pet**, it would be a bunny.

photograph *photographs*

These are **photographs** of Franklin's summer vacation.

piano

Granny is teaching Franklin to play the **piano**. It takes lots of practice!

pick *picks, picked, picking*

Franklin and Bear are **picking** berries.

picnic

The mice are having a **picnic** under the park bench.

picture

Franklin drew a **picture** of everyone in his neighborhood.

pie

It's fly **pie** — fresh from the oven. Yum!

piece

Who will get the first **piece** of birthday cake?

pirate *pirates*

Franklin, Rabbit, Bear and Snail are dressed up as **pirates**.

plant

Franklin's **plant** is finally starting to grow!

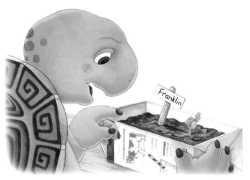

plate

Franklin's **plate** is empty. He's waiting for his dinner!

play *plays, played, playing*

Franklin is **playing** with Bear's sister, Beatrice.

playground

The **playground** is one of Franklin's favorite places.

point *points, pointed, pointing*

Mr. Owl is **pointing** to the sign.

pond

Franklin's friends are swimming in the **pond**.

pour *pours, poured, pouring*

Franklin's mother is **pouring** milk on Franklin's Fly Krispy cereal.

present *presents*

Who are all these **presents** for?

pretty

Beaver looks **pretty** in her ballet costume.

pull *pulls, pulled, pulling*

Franklin is **pulling** his wagon.

pumpkin

Franklin is choosing the perfect **pumpkin**.

push *pushes, pushed, pushing*

Franklin is **pushing** Harriet in her stroller.

put *puts, put, putting*

When Franklin is finished with something, he **puts** it away.

Qq

"Quiet, Bear. There are quite a lot of questions on this quiz!" whispered Franklin.

queen

Franklin has a turtle **queen** puppet.

quickly

Franklin wants to get to the park **quickly**. His friends are waiting for him.

quilt

The **quilt** from Bear's bed is freshly washed.

Rr

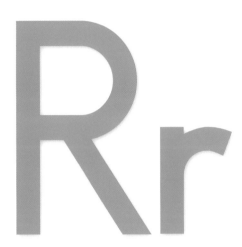

Beaver is reading and relaxing on her rubber raft.

rabbit

Rabbit is on his way to the bus stop.

raccoon

Look — **Raccoon** is waving hello!

race

The **race** is over. Franklin finally crossed the finish line!

rain

"**Rain**, **rain**, go away!" sings Franklin.

rainbow

After the storm, a beautiful **rainbow** appeared.

reach *reaches, reached, reaching*

Franklin is **reaching** for his cap.

read *reads, read, reading*

Bear likes to **read**.

ready

Franklin is **ready** to go to the hospital for his operation.

rest *rests, rested, resting*

Beaver, Goose and Duck are **resting** after the big race.

ride *rides, rode, riding*

Franklin is **riding** his bicycle without training wheels!

rocket

The Adventure Club made this **rocket** out of a big cardboard box.

roll *rolls, rolled, rolling*

Franklin's mother is **rolling** out the cookie dough.

room

Franklin is working on a project in his **room**.

rose

Franklin's mother has a **rose** garden.

run *runs, ran, running*

Franklin is **running** — he's in a hurry to meet his friends.

Ss

Franklin and Otter love to splash and swim in the summertime sun.

sad

Franklin is **sad**. He misses his old blue blanket.

salad

Ladybug **salad** is one of Franklin's favorite dishes.

school

This is Franklin's **school**.

scissors

Franklin has his own pair of **scissors** for arts and crafts.

season *seasons*

Franklin's picture shows the four **seasons**.

see *sees, saw, seeing*

Franklin's family came to **see** the school play.

seed

Franklin planted this **seed** for his school project. Soon it will be a plant.

set *sets, set, setting*

Harriet is helping her mother **set** the table.

sew *sews, sewed, sewing*

What is Franklin's mother **sewing**?

share *shares, shared, sharing*

Franklin is **sharing** his toy dog, Sam, with Harriet.

shell

When Franklin is afraid, he hides inside his **shell**.

shop *shops, shopped, shopping*

Franklin and his mother are **shopping** for fruits and vegetables.

show *shows, showed, showing*

Franklin is **showing** a picture of Raccoon's family to his father.

sick

Franklin stays home from school when he is **sick**.

sign

Beaver and Franklin made a **sign** for the Secret Adventure Club.

sister

Franklin is picking berries with his little **sister**, Harriet.

sit *sits, sat, sitting*

In the summer, Franklin and Bear spend time **sitting** on the dock.

skate *skates*

Franklin is carrying his **skates** on his shoulder.

skip *skips, skipped, skipping*

Beaver is very good at **skipping** rope.

skunk

Skunk is reading a booklet about the museum.

sled

Bear is pulling the **sled**.

sleep *sleeps, slept, sleeping*
Shh! Harriet is **sleeping** in her stroller.

slide *slides, slid, sliding*
The mice are **sliding** down the **slide**.

small
Snail is **small**, and the gift he brought to the town hall is **small**, too!

smile *smiles, smiled, smiling*
Franklin told Moose to **smile** for the camera.

snack
Franklin's mother is getting his after-school **snack** ready.

snail
Snail is Franklin's smallest friend.

snow

Franklin likes to make angels in the **snow**.

soft

Franklin's old blue blanket is very **soft**.

speak   *speaks, spoke, speaking*

Who is Bear **speaking** to on the telephone?

startled

Franklin and Snail were **startled** to bump into a dinosaur at the museum.

step   *steps*

Franklin is waiting for Fox on the library **steps**.

store

Franklin's father often shops at the hardware **store**.

storm

Franklin is afraid of the **storm** outside.

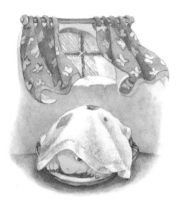

story   *stories*

Every night, Franklin's mother reads him two **stories**.

sun

The **sun** is setting. Soon it will be time for bed.

surprised

Franklin's father was **surprised** when a creepy hand tapped him on the shoulder.

swim   *swims, swam, swimming*

Badger can **swim** from one end of the pond to the other.

swing

Harriet loves it when Franklin pushes her on the **swing**.

T t

Franklin's trunk holds trucks, trains and toy turtles.

tail *tails*

Here are three different **tails** — a bushy **tail**, a flat **tail** and a striped **tail**.

take *takes, took, taking*

Franklin is **taking** pictures.

talk *talks, talked, talking*

Franklin and Beaver are **talking** about what to do after school.

tall

Franklin is growing up. Look at how **tall** he is now!

teach *teaches, taught, teaching*

Mr. Owl is **teaching** the class about the signs of spring.

teacher

Mr. Owl is Franklin's **teacher**.

team

Franklin's **team** is ready to play a great game of soccer!

telephone

Franklin's grandparents live far away, so he talks to them on the **telephone**.

tell *tells, told, telling*

What story is Beaver **telling** now?

tie *ties, tied, tying*

Franklin can **tie** his shoes.

time

What **time** is it on the turtle clock?
It's **time** to get up!

tired

Bear has been picking berries all day.
Now he is **tired**.

together

Franklin and Moose are making
a poster **together**.

tool *tools*

Franklin's parents keep their **tools** in
a toolbox.

top

Franklin is sleeping with his toy turtle
on **top** of his shell.

town

Franklin and his parents are going to the big Halloween party in **town**.

toy *toys*

Beaver has lots of **toys**, but her favorite **toy** is her teddy bear.

train

This is Franklin's toy **train**.

treat *treats*

Mmmm. Look at the **treats** for the Valentine's Day party!

tree *trees*

The **trees** change color in the fall.

truck

A big **truck** is moving all of Moose's things to his new house.

Uu

Bear will stay under his umbrella until the rain stops.

under

Goose has a great hiding place **under** the bridge!

up

Franklin is holding Sam **up** high so that Harriet can't reach him.

upset

Franklin is **upset** because he cannot find his valentines.

Vv

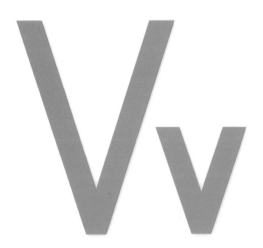

Franklin and Snail made a variety of very nice valentines.

vacation
For their summer **vacation**, Franklin and Bear are canoeing with their fathers.

vegetable *vegetables*
Franklin's mother served these **vegetables** at the Thanksgiving feast.

visit *visits, visited, visiting*
Franklin's mother and Harriet are **visiting** Dr. Bear and Beatrice.

Ww

Franklin's shell is wonderfully warm — he doesn't want to wake up!

walk *walks, walked, walking*

Franklin is **walking** to the park to play baseball.

warm

Raccoon's blanket keeps him **warm** on cold nights.

wash *washes, washed, washing*

Franklin is going to **wash** his blanket.

watch *watches, watched, watching*

Everyone is **watching** the school play.

water

Franklin's father is putting out the fire with **water**.

wave *waves, waved, waving*

Franklin is **waving** good-bye.

wear *wears, wore, wearing*

Franklin is **wearing** a soldier costume in the school play.

wet

Oh, no. Now Franklin's soccer ball is **wet**!

wheel *wheels*

Franklin wishes he could ride his bicycle without training **wheels**.

wheelbarrow

Franklin's father uses a **wheelbarrow** when he works in the garden.

win   *wins, won, winning*

Franklin's team was happy to **win** the soccer game.

wind

The **wind** is so strong that Franklin's umbrella turned inside out!

window

Franklin is watching for Bear at the **window**.

with

Franklin is eating pancakes **with** ladybugs.

without

Bear is eating pancakes **without** ladybugs.

wolf

Fire Chief **Wolf** helps keep Woodland safe.

woods

Uh-oh. Franklin is not supposed to go into the **woods** alone!

wonder *wonders, wondered, wondering*

"Hmmm. What could this present be?" Franklin **wonders**.

work *works, worked, working*

Franklin and his friends are **working** hard to fix up their clubhouse.

wood

Franklin collected **wood** for the fire.

write *writes, wrote, writing*

Franklin is **writing** a letter to the tooth fairy.

Xx

**Fox has a box
of excellent blocks.**

X ray

Dr. Bear is showing Franklin the **X ray** she took of his bones.

xylophone

Snail plays the **xylophone** in the school band.

89

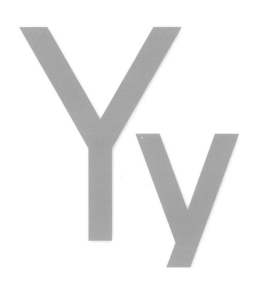

"Yay!" yelled Harriet.
"This year, I get a yummy
yellow birthday cake!"

yard

Franklin and his mother are playing catch in the front **yard**.

yawn *yawns, yawned, yawning*

Harriet is **yawning**. She needs a nap!

yo-yo

Bear can do tricks with his **yo-yo**.

Zz

Zip that zipper, Franklin!

zebra

Raccoon drew a picture of his favorite animal — a **zebra**.

zero

Franklin ate two fly cookies. Now there are **zero** cookies on his plate!

zigzag   *zigzags, zigzagged, zigzagging*

This frog is **zigzagging** his way across the lily pads.

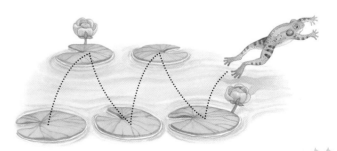

Numbers

1
one cecropia moth caterpillar

2
two monarch butterflies

3
three Clouded Sulphur butterflies

4
four water beetles

5
five dagger moths

6
six earwigs

7
seven grasshoppers

8
eight mayflies

9
nine red banded leafhoppers

10
ten wooly bear caterpillars

92

11
eleven damsel flies

12
twelve Karner blue butterflies

13
thirteen honeybees

14
fourteen locust borers

15
fifteen ladybugs

16
sixteen web weaver spiders

17
seventeen caddis flies

18
eighteen asparagus beetles

19
nineteen carpenter ants

20
twenty houseflies

Days of the Week

What a busy week! Franklin keeps a journal to record
what he does every day. Here is a page out of his journal.

Monday

On my way to Fox's house, I got
soaked in a rainstorm. It was so windy,
my umbrella turned inside out!

Tuesday

Today is my birthday! My party was
last Saturday, but this morning I got up
early for a special pancake breakfast.

Wednesday

My plant finally sprouted at school!
Mr. Owl thinks it is going to be the tallest,
strongest plant in the class!

Thursday

After school, I went to visit Dr. Bear for
my yearly checkup. She said that I have
grown two inches since last year!

94

Friday

My class went on a trip to the museum.
We saw scary dinosaurs and got to
dress up in knights' armor!

Yahoo! It's the weekend!

Saturday

Bear came for a sleepover. Dad built a big
campfire outside and we roasted wieners. We're
going to camp out in the living room tonight!

Sunday

I scored a goal in the big soccer game!
My team played really well. After the game,
we all went out for ice cream to celebrate.

Months of the Year

January

It's time to shovel
the walk again.

February

Franklin is getting ready
for Valentine's Day.

March

Uh-oh, Harriet! Watch
out for the mud!

July

School is out. Everyone
to the pond!

August

Have fun at day camp,
Franklin.

September

Back to school!

April

It smells like spring!

May

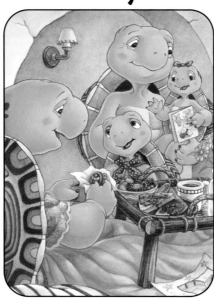

Happy Mother's Day!

June

Summer is here!

October

Mummies and monsters and ghosts — oh my!

November

Brrr! It's getting chilly.

December

Special decorations for a special time of year.

Seasons in Woodland

The classroom bulletin board is decorated to celebrate the four seasons in Woodland. Some of Mr. Owl's students have drawn pictures of their favorite time of year. Who do you think each picture belongs to?

SPRING

SUMMER

FALL

WINTER

Parts of a Turtle

Some parts of Franklin's body look like yours, and some parts look quite different. What does Franklin have that you don't have? What do you have that Franklin doesn't have?

eyelid
eye
head

nose
nostril

mouth
tongue
fingernail
thumb
finger
hand

neck
shoulder

wrist
arm
elbow

carapace
(back of shell)

plastron
(front of shell)

leg
knee

ankle

heel
foot
toenail

Words I Can Read

How many of these words can you read?
Keep practicing as you work through each set.
The words that appear in green are words that
you can find in this dictionary.

Set 1 — Preschool

a	I	run
and	in	said
away	is	see
big	it	the
blue	jump	three
can	little	to
come	look	two
down	make	up
find	me	we
for	my	where
funny	not	yellow
go	one	you
help	play	
here	red	

Set 2 — Kindergarten

all	he	that
am	into	there
are	like	they
at	must	this
ate	new	too
be	no	under
black	now	want
brown	on	was
but	our	well
came	out	went
cow	pleased	what
did	pretty	white
do	ran	who
eat	ride	will
four	say	with
get	she	yes
good	so	
have	soon	

Set 3 — First Grade

after	has	over
again	her	put
an	him	round
any	his	some
as	how	stop
ask	just	take
by	know	thank
could	let	them
every	live	think
fly	may	walk
from	of	were
give	old	when
going	once	
had	open	

Set 4 — Second Grade

always	goes	these
because	green	those
been	ground	upon
before	its	us
best	made	use
both	many	very
buy	off	wash
call	or	which
cold	pull	why
does	read	wish
don't	right	work
fast	sing	would
first	sit	your
five	sleep	
found	tell	
gave	their	

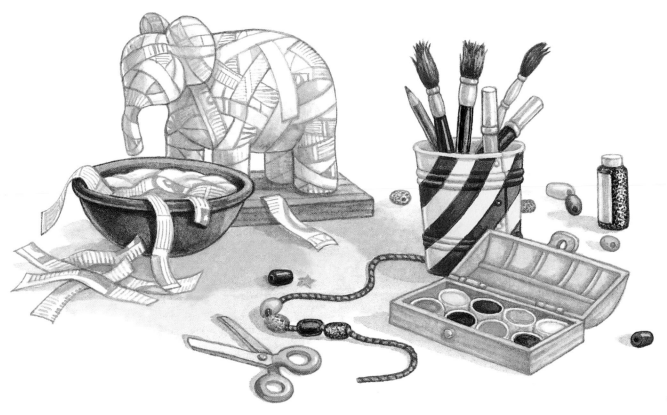

How to Use This Book

Before you begin using the dictionary with the child, take a tour of its features!

Alphabet Line

The dictionary is organized into sections based on the letters of the alphabet. Read along the alphabet line as you browse through the dictionary or as you search for a particular word. The highlighted letter indicating the current section will help the child know whether to go forward or backward to find a word.

Letter Header

Each section is introduced by a header sentence with an illustration. These sentences provide a story-based introduction to the letter and use an alliterative technique that draws the child into the section. As you read these sentences together, ask the child to think of other words that start with the same letter and to create a new alliterative sentence.

a b c d e f g h i j k l m

Cc

Clothes, costumes and clutter —
time to clean the closet!

cake
Granny is making a birthday **cake** for Franklin's mother.

call   *calls, called, calling*
Franklin is **calling** Bear on the telephone.

camera
Franklin found a **camera**. Hmmm. Who does it belong to?

Illustration

The friendly, familiar illustrations provide a natural link to the Franklin storybooks. Avid Franklin fans will enjoy revisiting favorite stories and characters. Talk about who is in each illustration and what's happening in the scene as you explore words and new concepts with the child.

n o p q r s t u v w x y z

camp *camps, camped, camping*
Franklin and Bear are **camping** out in the living room.

can *cans*
Tin **cans** make great play telephones!

candle *candles*
When the lights go out during a storm, Franklin's mother lights **candles**.

candy
Franklin's father is enjoying his valentine **candy**.

cap
Franklin often wears his red baseball **cap**.

card
Who is this valentine **card** for?

17

Word Entry

Each word entry is presented using a simple explanative sentence that allows even the youngest reader to develop and extend vocabulary concepts. Encourage the child to match the main word entry to the word in bold type in the sentence. This can be tricky as the tense changes for some verbs.

Question Entry

Some entries are given in a question format. The purpose of this format is not to determine a correct answer, but to encourage discussion. The illustration often provides clues to possible answers. In some cases, the child might recognize the illustration as being from a Franklin story. This is an opportunity for the child to reflect on a previously read story while considering the question.

Language Learning

Franklin's Picture Dictionary is a language-learning resource. It supports the development of concepts related to word meaning and usage, as well as the development of a variety of early reading and writing skills.

Spoken Language: Word Usage and Comprehension

The dictionary has been designed especially for children in kindergarten to third grade, with a focus on the following language objectives:

- to increase vocabulary

- to develop the ability to use words with confidence and expertise

- to explore basic grammar structures such as nouns, verbs, adjectives and adverbs

Written Language: Reading and Writing

Through informal experiences with the dictionary and participation in some of the suggested activities, children will begin to extend and refine their understanding of language and how it works, both in verbal and written form.

For the younger audience, *Franklin's Picture Dictionary* provides a theme-based environment that encourages the development of such early literacy skills as

- alphabetization

- early reading, aided by the linking of pictorially expressed ideas and their corresponding text

- familiarity with techniques for using a dictionary

- the ability to obtain meaning from written text

For the older audience, *Franklin's Picture Dictionary* acts as a treasury of ideas and a source of words that will assist children as they

- acquire greater independent reading skills

- refer to models of correct word usage in their personal writing

- identify and use the correct spellings of words

- experiment with more complex writing styles in their personal writing by exploring the alliterative samples provided on the letter-header pages

A Wealth of Words to Discover

The word entries in the dictionary were selected for inclusion based on a number of criteria, including whether they are

- common words in the English language

- high-frequency words*

- words encountered in Franklin storybooks

- words whose meanings can be effectively conveyed through illustrations

Types of Words

A variety of word types have been included in this dictionary so that children can begin to explore the different parts of speech. Where appropriate, variations of words (plurals and verb variations) are included beside the main word.

noun
word that names a person, place or thing

verb
word that names an action

adjective
word that describes a person, place or thing

adverb
word that describes an action

preposition
word that describes the position of something or someone

*High-frequency words that are difficult to illustrate have not been included as main word entries. A full listing of high-frequency words can be found in the "Words I Can Read" section starting on page 100.

Suggested Activities

Reading skills develop at an individual rate based on experience, maturity, motivation and personal learning needs. For this reason, activities with varying levels of difficulty are suggested in the following pages. Activity ideas for both the younger reader and the more experienced reader are provided, all of which will be most effective with adult participation or supervision. Start where the child is most comfortable and explore more challenging activities as appropriate. Review the concepts frequently, and as skill and confidence develop, encourage the child to take the lead in reading and exploring the ideas presented.

Alphabetization

Knowing the position of each letter in the alphabet helps the child effectively use a dictionary. Here are some activities to reinforce this skill.

Musical Letters

Sing the alphabet song together while following along the alphabet line at the top of the page. As you sing, stop at different letters. Ask the child to find a page in the dictionary that corresponds to the chosen letter. Allow the child to take a turn being the singer while you locate the correct page in the book.

Letter Locator

Have the child choose a word on any page in the dictionary. Then, while referring to the alphabet line, ask "Is the first letter of this word near the beginning, the middle or the end?" Repeat this activity often to help the child become more familiar with and confident of the position of each letter in the alphabet.

Before or After?

Have the child turn to any page in the dictionary. Look at the alphabet line at the top of the page. Help the child identify which letter is highlighted in the line. Then ask the child to find the page where the word **basket** (or any other word in the dictionary that begins with a letter other than the one highlighted) appears. Ask "What letter does the word **basket** begin with? Does the letter B come before or after the page that is currently displayed?" Be sure to refer to the alphabet line if necessary.

Back in Order

For the older child, review the order of the alphabet and discuss how this organization lets us order words in a dictionary. When appropriate, discuss how the second and third letters of a word also help determine its placement in a dictionary. Practice organizing small groups of words in alphabetical order. Choose four or five words from the dictionary and write each on a strip of paper. To begin, order by initial letter. Then, when more of a challenge is required, order by first and second letters, and so on.

Word Meanings

Children of varying reading levels can grasp meaning from the sentences provided for each word in *Franklin's Picture Dictionary*. Younger readers will enjoy exploring the illustrations and, with support and guidance, can begin to link the corresponding pictures and words. Experienced readers will enjoy the child-friendly language.

The following activities will help the child to better understand the words and their corresponding meanings and to figure out the meanings of unfamiliar words.

Words I Know

As an introduction to words and their meanings, compile a list of familiar words from the dictionary. Write each on a strip of paper. Look up the words in the dictionary and take turns reading the meanings.

Ask the younger child to choose any word in the dictionary and make up a definition or sentence that describes what the word means. Remind the child to refer to the illustration while coming up with this definition. Read the dictionary sentence together and see how it matches the idea expressed by the child. Alternatively, ask the child to use the word in a sentence.

Mystery Word

Ask the younger child to turn to a particular page in the dictionary (e.g., page 21). Say that you're thinking of a word that names "something that Bear needs when he picks berries" (or a definition of another word that appears on the page). Ask the child to point to the matching word entry (**basket**), and then help him read the word and corresponding sentence.

For the older child, do not identify the page number. Instead, say "I'm thinking of a word that begins with B, and it is something that Bear needs when he picks berries." The child will then turn to the relevant section and locate the corresponding entry.

More than One

Discuss how a word's meaning can change when you add **s** or **es**, making the word mean more than one. Notice that for some nouns the plural form has been identified beside the main word entry (e.g., **apples**, **blueberries**). This occurs when the word is used in its plural form in the corresponding sentence. Point out to the child that simply adding an **s** doesn't always work. To demonstrate this, ask the child to look up **mouse**, and note that the plural doesn't follow the regular "add an **s**" rule (**mice**). Pluralize other nouns in the dictionary and discuss how their meaning is now two or more.

Different Endings

Encourage the child to experiment with making new words by adding different endings to the main word entry. Start by looking up different verbs to see how endings are added to make new words. Differentiate between sentences that use the word in its base form (e.g., Bear is helping Franklin **feed** Goldie) and others that use a variation of the base word in the sentence (e.g., Franklin is good at **diving** into the pond). Ask the child to locate a favorite verb and make up a sentence using the verb in a different form. Try the same activity using adjectives (e.g., tall, taller, tallest).

Word Types

When exploring the different parts of speech with younger children, it is not necessary to refer to terms such as nouns, verbs, adjectives and adverbs. A simple discussion about the different purposes of words (to name things, to describe actions) is a good starting point. Use the following suggestions to help the child form an understanding of the different kinds of words.

Words That Name Characters

Help the child develop an understanding of nouns by explaining that some words name people, places or things. Ask the child to name some of the characters he has seen in Franklin's world. Then ask the child to locate each of the following names in the dictionary:

- Badger
- Moose
- Raccoon
- Bear
- Otter
- Skunk
- Beaver
- Mr. Owl
- Snail
- Fox
- Rabbit

Words That Name Family Members

Continuing with words that name people, ask the child to find the word **mother** in the dictionary. Look up these other words that name people in a family:

- aunt
- father
- mom
- brother
- grandparents
- parents
- dad
- granny
- sister

Words That Name Places

Ask the child to find the word **hospital** in the dictionary. Look up these other words that name places in Franklin's town of Woodland and the child's community:

- library
- playground
- school
- market
- pond
- woods
- museum

Words That Name Actions

Ask the child to think of things that Franklin and his friends can do (e.g., Franklin can **kick** a soccer ball). Explain that **kick** is an action word. Ask "What other words can you find in the dictionary that name an action?" There are more than 200! Ask what action words describe things that the child can do.

Words That Are Opposites

To reinforce the concept of opposites, have the child turn to a particular page (e.g., page 9). Then ask "What word means the opposite of **asleep**?" The child will then think of the word **awake** and locate it on the same page. The following opposites can be found in the dictionary:

- awake/asleep
- big/little
- cold/hot
- cool/warm
- down/up
- dry/wet
- empty/full
- everybody/nobody
- good/bad
- inside/outside
- new/old
- over/under
- push/pull
- sad/happy
- with/without

Words That Describe Feelings

Some words describe how people feel. Usually, Franklin is **happy**, but sometimes he's not. Ask the child to think of other words that describe how a person can feel. Look up the following words in the dictionary and ask the child what might have happened to make the character feel that way:

- afraid
- eager
- sad
- angry
- excited
- startled
- annoyed
- grouchy
- surprised
- disappointed
- mad
- upset

Words That Describe Positions

Ask the child to look up the word **between**. Discuss how this word describes where Franklin is sitting. Ask the child to think of other words that describe the position of something or someone. The following words can be found in the dictionary:

- above
- into
- over
- along
- on
- under
- beside
- out
- with
- inside
- outside
- without

Reading

In addition to being a wonderful resource for exploring the nature of words and expanding vocabulary, *Franklin's Picture Dictionary* offers engaging text for the younger child to develop early reading skills and for the older child to acquire independent reading skills.

The text is simple but meaningful, as it relates very closely to each illustration. Many of the word entries retell an event that has occurred in a Franklin story, using child-friendly language. For those who are familiar with Franklin and his adventures, this dictionary provides a supportive reading resource where the child can learn to read independently while learning more about Franklin, his friends, his family and his community. For children experiencing Franklin for the first time, the mini-stories provide an introduction to Franklin's world, which can then be further explored by reading some of the storybooks.

Depending on the child's reading ability, reading activities will vary. As a guideline for all children, remember to encourage the child to read the words with you and to take over the reading when able to do so. Here are some other suggestions for focusing on reading skills.

Decoding the Words

When beginning a new section, read the letter header with the child. Point out the key words and the letter they begin with.

Encourage the child to refer to the illustrations when trying to identify unknown words.

Words I Can Read

Help the child keep an inventory of all the words that she can read. Refer to the list of high-frequency words on pages 100–101 to practice reading the sight words that the child will encounter frequently in this dictionary and in other materials for children.

Franklin Storybooks

Read a Franklin storybook together and discuss the meaning of unfamiliar words.

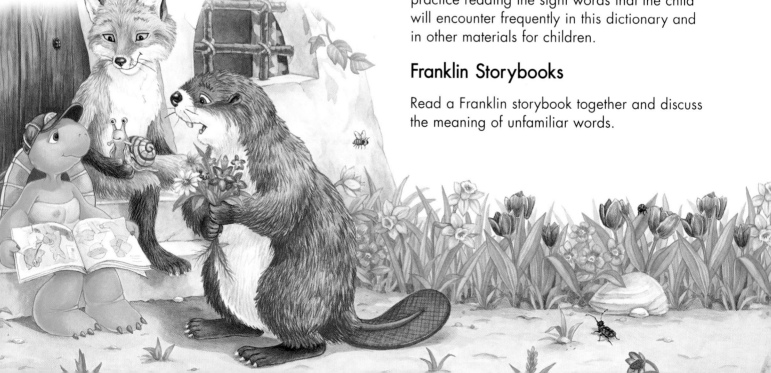

Creative Writing

The simple, child-friendly language used in *Franklin's Picture Dictionary* is an excellent writing model for both the younger child who is just beginning to write independently and the more experienced writer. There are several writing activities that can be introduced to children of varying abilities using the dictionary as a model.

Personal Dictionary

Help the child make a picture dictionary of favorite words or of the family. Cut out pictures from catalogs or use photos taken for this purpose. Mount the pictures in a scrapbook with the target letter written in large print on the left-hand side of the page. Have the child write a definition or sentence for each word.

Word Bank

Encourage the child to create a list (or word bank) that includes words needed for writing. This will help to support spelling skills, as well as organizational and classification skills.

Alliteration Challenge

Referring to the more complex sentences presented on the letter-header pages, challenge the child to create a sequence of words all beginning with the same initial letter (e.g., *Dapper Dan the dog daringly drags the drapes down to the dangerous Danube*).